Crystal Pegasus

Special Collector's Edition
First Time in Print: Part 1 *and* Part 2

Creator, Writer, Art Director and Project Leader: Tom Marcoux

Associate Art Director: Johanna E. Mac Leod

Part 1 Character and Background Illustrator: Natsu Sakamichi

Part 2 Character Illustrator: Katie Halbert

Part 2 Background Illustrator and Art Direction Consultant: Becca J.G. England

Part 2 Preliminary Sketch Designer: Kira Marriner

Colorists: Sarah Barrie Fenton, Abby Lee, Christopher Allen Loe, Lindsay Morita

Crystal Pegasus Created By Tom Marcoux

Find out the Latest News on Crystal Pegasus and Rose, the Good Dragon at:

www.facebook.com/CrystalPegasusandRose

www.CrystalPegasusMovie.com

For more copies, book readings and performances: tomsupercoach@gmail.com

Tom Marcoux

Writer, Art Director, Cover Designer and Project Leader

Johanna E. Mac Leod

Associate Art Director and Image Retoucher

Natsu Sakamichi

Part 1 Character and Background Illustrations

Katie Halbert

Cover Character Illustrations, "Welcome" Page Character Illustrations,
Part 2 Character Illustrations, Caption Placement, PDF Assembly,
Colorist For "Welcome" Page and Additional Image Retouching

Becca J.G. England

Cover Background Illustration, Part 2 Background Illustrations and Art Direction Consultant

Sarah Barrie Fenton

Colorist For Pages: 1, 2, 3, 4, 5, 6, 7, 8, 9, 10, 11, 12, 13, 14, 15, 16, 17, 18, 19, 40, 42, 47, 48,
49, 50, 57, 60, 61, 63, 64, 65, 66, 69, 70, 72, 75, 77, 82, the "Part 2" cover and the Front Cover

Abby Lee

Colorist For Pages: 29, 30, 31, 32, 33, 34, 35, 36, 37, 38, 39, 43, 44, 45,
46, 51, 52, 53, 54, 55, 56, 62, 71, 74 (page 74 Repeated On Back Cover), 78, 81

Christopher Allan Loe

Colorists For Pages: 20, 21, 22, 23, 24, 25, 26, 27, 28, 58, 67, 68, 73, 76, 79

Kira Marriner

Preliminary Sketch Design

Lindsay Morita

Colorist For Pages: 59 and 80

Note: Suzanne Fiore contributed additional preliminary sketchs during her internship.

PART 1

ONCE THERE WAS A PONY NAMED DE'MAR WHO HAD A LITTLE BROTHER NAMED DUCKY.

ILLUSTRATED BY: NATSU SAKAMICHI

ONE NIGHT, DE'MAR AND DUCKY SETTLED DOWN TO SLEEP NEAR THEIR MOTHER, MOMMA SHEEP.

SHE HAD ADOPTED THEM.

NONE OF THEM KNEW OF THE MAGIC APPROACHING THEIR BARN.

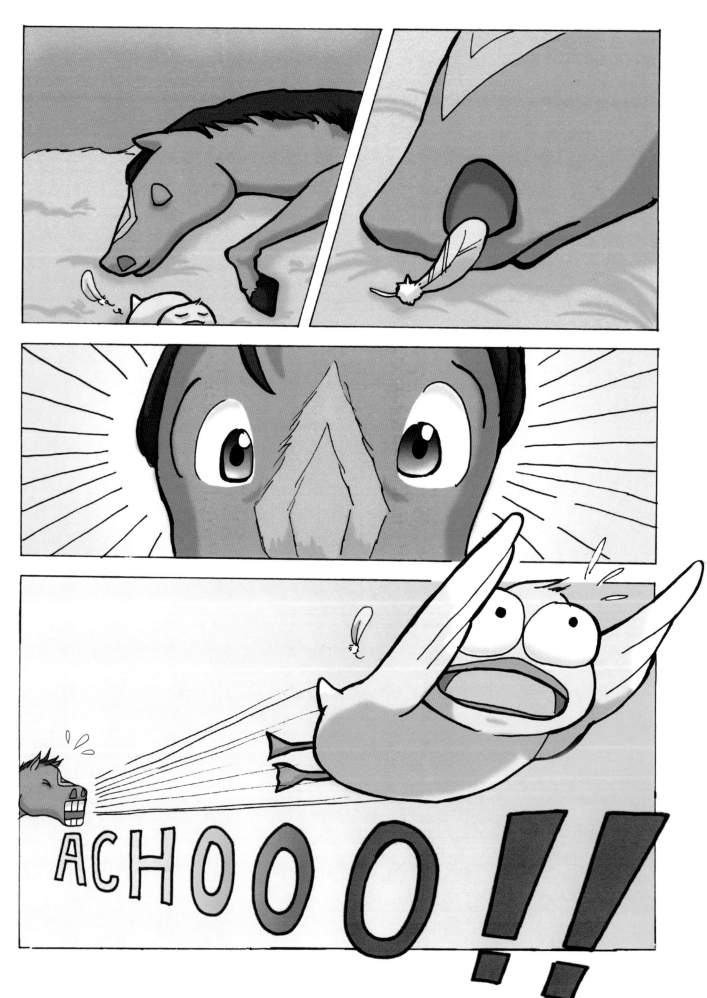

ACHOOO!!

MAYOR ROOSTER WAS ANGRY.

DE'MAR, YOU MUST RETURN THOSE WINGS TO WHOMEVER THEY BELONG!

AFTER HIM!

HOW CAN I
HELP DE'MAR?

16

DE'MAR FELL INTO THE ENCHANTED LAKE.

YOU'RE THE WEIRDEST LOOKING THING I'VE EVER SEEN!

THE MOCKING BIRD LANDED ON DE'MAR'S NOSE.

GOOD! I KNEW YOU COULD DO IT!

DE'MAR!

CRYSTAL PEGASUS
PART 2

WRITTEN BY: TOM MARCOUX
ART DIRECTOR AND PROJECT LEADER: TOM MARCOUX
ASSISTANT ART DIRECTOR: JOHANNA E. MAC LEOD
CHARACTER ILLUSTRATIONS: KATIE HALBERT
BACKGROUND ILLUSTRATIONS: BECCA J.G. ENGLAND
COLORISTS: SARAH BARRIE FENTON, ABBY LEE,
CHRISTOPHER ALLAN LOE, LINDSAY MORITA

ROSE ZIPPED PAST CRYSTAL PEGASUS AND HIS LITTLE BROTHER DUCKY.

WHOOSH

IT'S A GIRL DRAGON!

A RUDE GIRL DRAGON.

SHENDIK REMEMBERED HIS BIG MISTAKE. IT BEGAN
AS HE STOOD BENEATH THE PORTRAIT OF HIS FATHER...

DRAGON KING ARRIVED ON THE FARM WITH HIS RHIGER SOLDIERS...
DRAGON KING, PLEASE DON'T...
OUT OF MY WAY!
WHACK

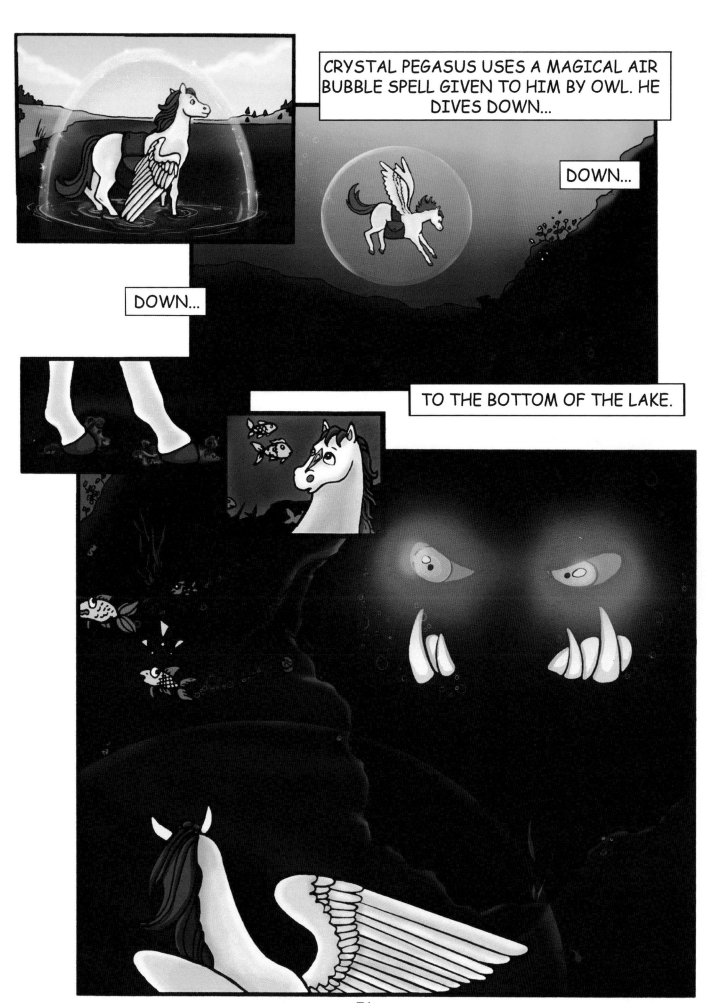

52

62

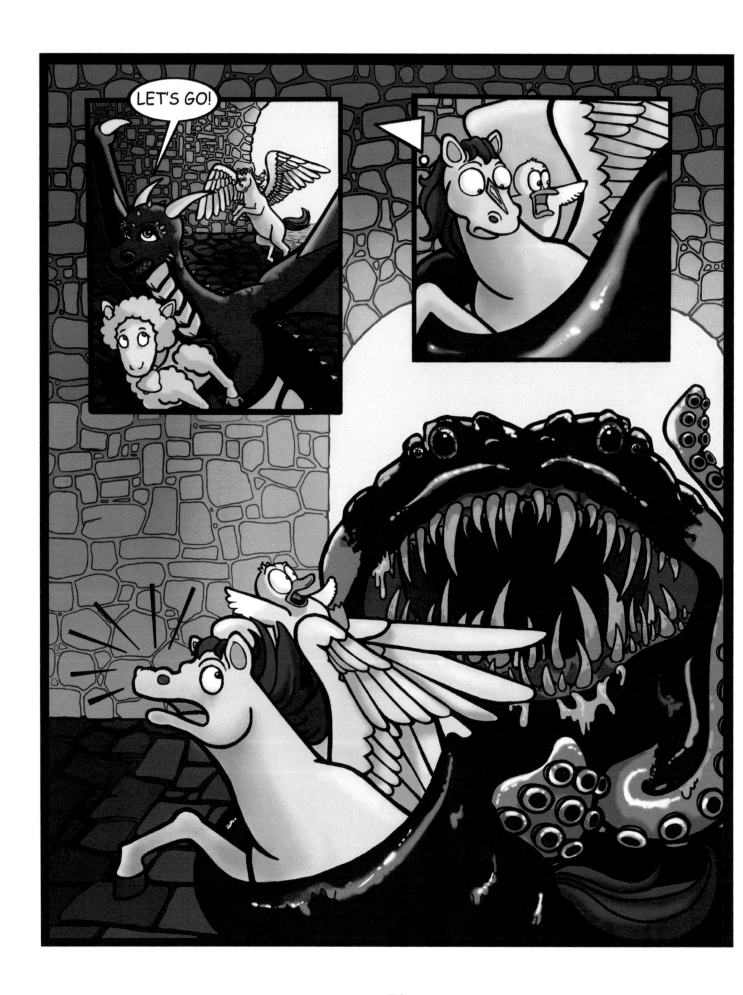

73

81

THE END...
OF THIS ADVENTURE.

Thanks for reading Crystal Pegasus Volume 1 and please

be sure to watch for Crystal Pegasus Volumes 2 and 3 in the future!

In the Appendix pages that follow, see artwork

by a number of Crystal Pegasus artists.

Thank you.

Become a Fan and Discover the Latest News on the

Trilogy, Webisodes and Feature Films at:

www.facebook.com/CrystalPegasusandRose

and

www.CrystalPegasusMovie.com

(also discover Crystal Pegasus and Rose t-shirts, toys and more)

YOU MEAN
THERE'S MORE?

Becca England

artgirl14@hotmail.com (408) 204-9423

Make Your Dreams Come True.

If your mom had to fight your first crayon out of your hand at bedtime, it's clear you are meant to be an artist. That's how it was for me. By Preschool, I was already telling everyone that I wanted to make the pictures in children's books. In the fourth grade, a school teacher suggested I look into the Academy of Art University. I came home and told my mom that I knew where I was going to college. Now my dream is my reality.

Katie Halbert

I was born in 1986 in San Jose, California. As soon as I was old enough to hold a pencil, I promptly began covering every available surface with doodles and stickers. Naturally enough, I ended up at The Academy of Art University in San Francisco. Crystal Pegasus is the first project I took on after graduating.

SELF PORTRAIT
Painted for a homework assignment a few years ago.

EARLY ROSE DESIGN
I'm not sorry we decided against this version. She'd have taken forever to draw.

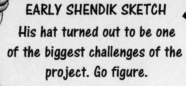

EARLY SHENDIK SKETCH
His hat turned out to be one of the biggest challenges of the project. Go figure.

KIRA MARRINER

Become a Fan and Discover the Latest News on the Crystal Pegasus Trilogy, Webisodes and Feature Films at www.facebook.com/CrystalPegasusandRose

and www.CrystalPegasusMovie.com

(also discover Crystal Pegasus and Rose t-shirts, toys and more)

For more copies of this book, book readings and performances, contact:

tomsupercoach@gmail.com

Crystal Pegasus

Created by Tom Marcoux

About The Author

   Tom Marcoux won a special award at the Emmy Awards. He wrote, directed, produced and acted in a feature film that went to Cannes film market, where it gained international distribution. In addition to *Crystal Pegasus* (children's fantasy), Marcoux created the graphic novel series *TimePulse* (science fiction) www.facebook.com/timepulsegraphicnovel and www.TimePulse.com

   Marcoux has written books on film directing, acting, and making a pitch for Film/Television. He also helps people like you fulfill big dreams. Known as America's Communication Coach, Marcoux has authored 16 books with sales in 15 countries. One of his books rose to #1 on Amazon Hot New Releases List for Business Communication (and Business Life). Marcoux guides clients and audiences (IBM, Sun Microsystems, and more) to success in job interviewing, public speaking, media relations, and branding. A member of the National Speakers Association, he is a professional coach and guest expert on TV, radio, and print, and was dubbed "the Personal Branding Instructor" by the *San Francisco Examiner*. He addressed six annual National Association of Broadcasters' Conferences. With a degree in psychology, Marcoux is a guest lecturer at Stanford University, DeAnza College, and California State University, and teaches public speaking and science fiction & fantasy at Academy of Art University. Visit www.TomSuperCoach.com to see how Tom coaches people to get more done using Time-Leverage. Visit Tom's blog at www.BeHeardandBeTrusted.com

Made in the USA
Lexington, KY
19 November 2012